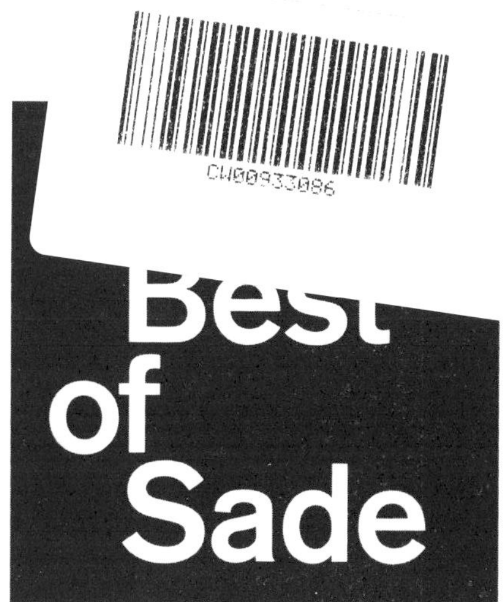

All the songs from the album
arranged for voice, piano & guitar

Includes lyrics & guitar chords

This publication is not authorised for sale in
the United States of America and/or Canada

Sony Music Publishing

Exclusive Distributors:
Music Sales Limited
8/9 Frith Street, London W1V 5TZ, England.
Music Sales Pty Limited
120 Rothschild Avenue, Rosebery, NSW 2018, Australia.

Order No. AM92663
ISBN 0-7119-4743-0

Your Guarantee of Quality:
As publishers, we strive to produce every book to the highest commercial standards.
Whilst endeavouring to retain the original running order of the soundtrack album, this book has been carefully designed to minimise awkward page turns and to make playing from it a real pleasure.
Particular care has been given to specifying acid-free, neutral-sized paper made from pulps which have not been elemental chlorine bleached.
This pulp is from farmed sustainable forests and was produced with special regard for the environment.
Throughout, the printing and binding have been planned to ensure a sturdy, attractive publication which should give years of enjoyment. If your copy fails to meet our high standards, please inform us and we will gladly replace it.

Printed and bound in Great Britain by
Caligraving Limited Thetford Norfolk

Your love is king

Words & Music: Adu & Matthewman

Dmaj7
Amaj7
Dmaj7
Nev-er need to part,
rul-er of my heart,
your kiss-es ring
round and round and round my head
Bm7
C♯m7
Dmaj7
C♯m7
touch-ing the ve-ry part of me that's mak-ing my soul sing,
I'm
I'm
Bm7
C♯m7
Dmaj9
Dmaj9
tear-ing the ve-ry heart of me. I'm cry-ing out for more. Your love is
cry-ing out for more,
your love is king.
Amaj7
Dmaj7
I'm com-ing up,
I'm

Amaj7
Dmaj7
Amaj7
com - ing.
You're mak-ing me dance
Dmaj7
Amaj7
Dmaj7
in - side.
Your love is
3
Dmaj9
Bm7
C♯m7
cry-ing out for more.
Touch-ing the ve-ry part of me that's
Dmaj7
C♯m7
Bm7
C♯m7
Dmaj9
mak-ing my soul sing,
I'm cry-ing out for more,
your love is king.

Amaj7
Dmaj7
This is no blind faith, this is
(2nd ad lib.) gotta crown you with my heart. (your love is
go.)
Amaj7
Dmaj7
Amaj7
no sad or sor-ry dream this is no
king) never, never need to part (your love is king) oh,
1
Dmaj7
Bm7
C#m7
Dmaj7
E11
blind faith. Your love your love is real.
2
Dmaj7
Amaj7
E11
3° to Fade
touch me, your love is king, nev - er let - ting

Hang on to your love

Words & Music: Adu & Matthewman

B♭maj7/D
Am7/D
eas - y to walk out on love. Take your time when the
eas - y when you're in love. Don't be a-shamed when the
B♭maj7/D
go-ing gets tough, it's so pre-cious.
go-ing gets tough, it's not eas - y, (don't give up) So if you
Am7/D
B♭maj7/D
want it to get strong-er you'd bet-ter not let go, you've got to hold on long-er if you
Am7/D
B♭maj7/D
want your love to grow. got to stick to-geth-er hand in glove, hold on tight, don't fight,

Am
Am7/D
Bb maj7/D
hang on to your love. In hea-ven's name why are you walk-ing a-way,
hang on to your love.
In hea - ven's name why do you play these games,
To Coda
D.%. al Coda
CODA
hang on to your love.
So if you
When you
Ad lib. to fade
find a love
find your love
don't let it walk a - way.
you've got to make it stay.
When you

Smooth operator

Words & Music: Adu & St. John

G
Dm7
high in the sky,
hea-ven
help him
when he falls.
Dm7
Am7
Gm7
Dia-mond life,
lov-er boy,
he
move in space with
min-i-mum waste
and max-i-mum joy.

Dm7
Am7
Gm7
Am7
Dm7
Am7
Ci - ty lights and busi - ness nights,
Face to face each clas - sic case,
Gm7
Am7
Dm7
Am7
Gm7
Am7
when you re - quire street - car de - sire for
we shad - ow box and dou - ble cross yet
Dm7
Am7
Gm7
Am7
Gm7
high - er heights. No place for be -
need the chase. A li - cence to
Am7
Dm7
gin - ners or sen - si - tive hearts,
love, in - sur - ance to hold,

Gm7
Am7
Dm7
when sen - ti - ment is left to chance,
melt all your mem-'ries and change in - to gold,
Gm7
Am7
no place to be end-ing but some-where to
his eyes are like an-gels but his heart is
Dm7
start.
cold.
Dm7
Am7
No need to ask he's a smooth op-er-at-or,
Gm7
Am7
Dm7
Am7
Gm7
Am7
Dm7
Am7
smooth op-er at-or,
smooth op-er-at-or,

Gm7
Am7
Dm7
Am7
Gm7
Am7
smooth op - er - at - or.
Dm7
Am7
Gm7
Am7
Dm7
Am7
Coast to coast, L. A. to Chi - ca - go, west-ern male.
Gm7
Am7
Dm7
Am7
Gm7
Am7
A - cross the north and south to Key Lar - go,
1 Dm7
Am7
Gm7
Am7
2 Dm7
Am7
Gm7
Am7
D.S. to fade
love for sale
love for sale.

Jezebel

Words & Music: Adu & Matthewman

Moderately
Dm7
/C
Gm7
(1.) Je - ze - bel
was-n't born
with a sil - ver
B♭-5
A7
Dm7
/C
spoon in her mouth,
she pro - bably had
less than ev - 'ry one of
Gm7
B♭-5
A7
Gm9
us.
But
when she knew

C6
Dm9
how to walk, she knew how to bring the house down,-can't
Gm9
C6
Bb-5
blame her for her beau-ty, she wins with her hands down.
1.
A
2.
A
Gm9
Reach for the top
3
C6
Dm9
and the sun is gon-na shine. Ev-'ry

Gm9
C6
Bb-5
win - ter was a war, she said I want to get what's mine.
1.
A
Dm7
/C
Jez - e - bel,
Gm9
Bb-5
A
Dm7
Jez-e - bel,
won't try to de - ny where she came from.
/C
Gm9
Bb-5
A
you can see it in her pride,
and the ra- ven in her eyes,

VERSE 2:
Jezebel, what a belle
Looks like a princess in her new dress
How did you get that
Do you really want to know she said
It would seem she's on her way
It's more, more than just a dream
She put on her stockings and shoes
Had nothing to lose - she said it was worth it.

The sweetest taboo

Words & Music: Adu & Ditcham

Gb
Fm7
Bbm7
Fm7
Gb
Fm7
sweet - est ta - boo;
Bbm7
Fm7
Gb
Fm7
Bbm7
Fm7
You give me, you're giv-ing me the sweet- est ta - boo. Too good for me.
Gb
Fm7
Bbm7
Fm7
Gb
Fm7
There's a qui- et storm and it nev- er felt like this be - fore.
Bbm7
Fm7
Gb
Fm7
Bbm7
Fm7
There's a qui- et storm that is you there's a qui- et storm and it

G♭
Fm7
B♭m7
Fm7
never felt this hot before, giving me something that's taboo
G♭
1° only
Fm7
B♭m7
Fm7
(Sometimes I think you're just too good for me.)
You give me the
G♭
Fm7
B♭m7
Fm7
G♭
Fm7
sweetest taboo, that's why I'm in love with you.
To Coda
B♭m7
Fm7
G♭
Fm7
B♭m7
Fm7
You give me the sweetest taboo sometimes I think you're just too good

Gb
Ab/Bb
for me.
I'd do an - y - thing for you
Ebm9
I'd stand out in the rain.
Ab/Bb
An - y - thing you want me to do,
don't let it slip a -
Ebm9
D.%. al Coda
way.

CODA
Bbm7
Fm7
Gb
too good for me,
you've got the big-gest heart,
some-times I think you're just too good for me.
Ev-'ry day is Christ-mas,
and ev-'ry night is New Year's Eve.
Will you keep on lov-ing me?

Bbm7
Fm7
Gb
Fm7
Bbm7
Fm7
Will you keep on, will you keep on,
Gb
Fm7
Bbm7
Fm7
bring - ing out — the best in me? —
Gb
Fm7
Bbm
Repeat to Fade

D.S.
There's a quiet storm
And it never felt this good before
There's a quiet storm
I think it's you
There's a quiet storm
And I never felt this hot before
Giving me something that's taboo.

Is it a crime?

Words & Music: Adu, Matthewman & Hale

Fm9
Cm7add4
I could see through all of your lies but still I miss you.
He takes her love but it does- n't
feel like mine, he tastes her kiss,
her kiss- es are not wine, they're not mine. He

Abmaj7
G7+
G7
Cm7add4
takes but sure-ly she can't give what I'm feeling now.
Db13+11
Abmaj7
G7
She takes, but sure-ly she does-n't
Cm7
F
Cm7
F
Cm7
CHORUS
Cm7add4
know how. Is it a crime,
Fm7
G+
1st Fret
G7
is it a crime, that I still

Cm7
Fm7
To Coda
want you, and I want you to want me too.
1.
G+
G7
1st Fret
(2.) My love is wid-
2.
D.%. al Coda
CODA
(%.) My love is wid-
It
dives and it jumps and it rip-ples like the
f
mf
deep-est o-cean. I can't give you more than that sure-ly you want me

VERSE 2:
My love is wider, wider than Victoria Lake
My love is taller, taller than the Empire State.

It dives and it jumps and it ripples like the deepest ocean
I can't give you more than that, surely you want me back.

D.S.
My love is wider than Victoria Lake
Taller than the Empire State
It dives and it jumps
I can't give you more than that, surely you want me back.

Never as good as the first time

Words & Music: Adu & Matthewman

Moderately fast ♩ = 108
F♯m
E/F♯
Bm7
mf
Verse
F♯m
E/F♯
Bm7
/F♯
1. Good times they come and they go, nev-er go - ing to know what fate is go - ing to blow
F♯m
your way; just hope_ that it feels right. Some-times it comes_ and it goes,

E/F♯
Bm7
/F♯
you take it ev - er so slow. And then you lose it, then it flows right to you.
F♯m
E/F♯
So we re - ly on the past, spe - cial mo - ments that last.
Bm7
/F♯
F♯m
Were they as ten-der as we dare to re - mem-ber? Such a fine time as this; what could
E/F♯
Bm7
/F♯
e - qual the bliss, the thrill of the first kiss. It - 'll

Chorus
Bm7
F♯m
blow right to you. It's nev - er as good as the first
time.
nev - er
as good as the first time.
1.
2.
F♯m9
(Vocal ad lib . . . .

Bm6
1,3,4. etc. Repeat ad lib. and Fade
2.
. . . . end vocal ad lib.)
F♯m
E/F♯
Nat - ural as the way we came to be.
Nat - ural as the way we came to be.
D/F♯
F♯m
Se - cond time
Se - cond time
E/F♯
D/F♯
1.
won't live up to the dream.
is not quite what it seemed.

VERSE 2:
Good times they come and they go,
Never going to know.
It's like the weather,
One day chicken, next day feathers.
The rose we remember, the thorns we forget;
We'd love and leave, never spend a minute on regret.

It is a possibility
The more we know the less we see.
Second time, second time is not quite what it seems.
Natural as the way we came to be;
Second time won't live up to the dream. *(To Chorus:)*

Love is stronger than pride

Words & Music: Adu, Hale & Matthewman

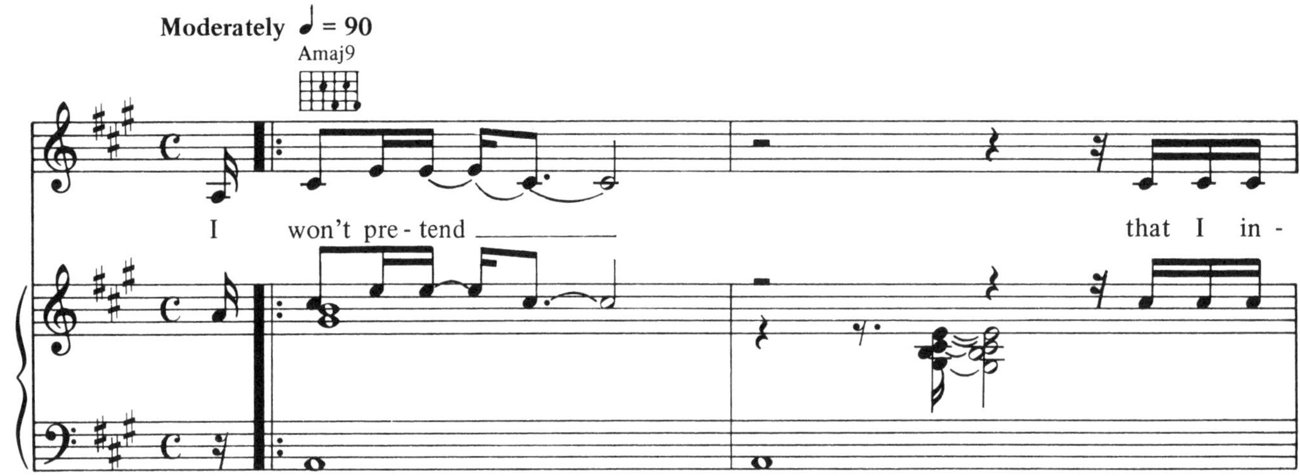
Moderately ♩ = 90
Amaj9
I won't pre - tend that I in -

E7sus4
Amaj9
tend to stop liv - ing. I won't pre - tend

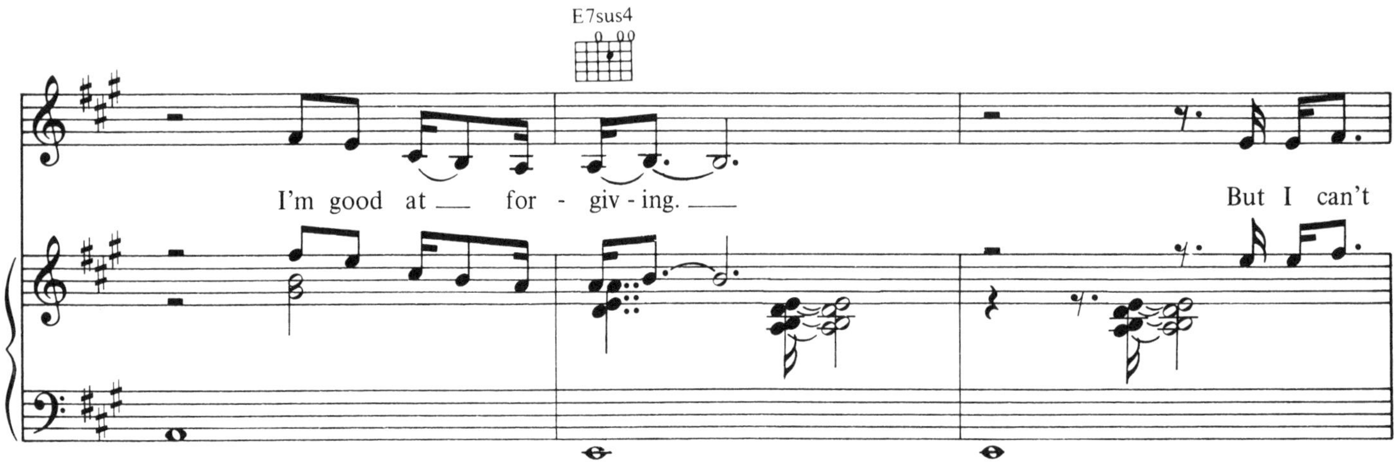
E7sus4
I'm good at for - giv - ing. But I can't

Amaj9
E7sus4
hate you although I have tried, mm.
Amaj9
I still really, really love you, love is
E7sus4
Amaj9
stronger than pride.
I still really, really love you,
E7sus4
1.
mm.
I

2.
Fmaj7/G
Sit - ting here wast-ing my time would be like
Sit - ting here wait-ing for you would be like
real - ly real - ly love you love is stronger than

Amaj9
Fmaj7/G
wait -ing for the sun to rise. It's all too clear,
wait -ing for winter. It's gonna be cold,
pride. I still really really love you

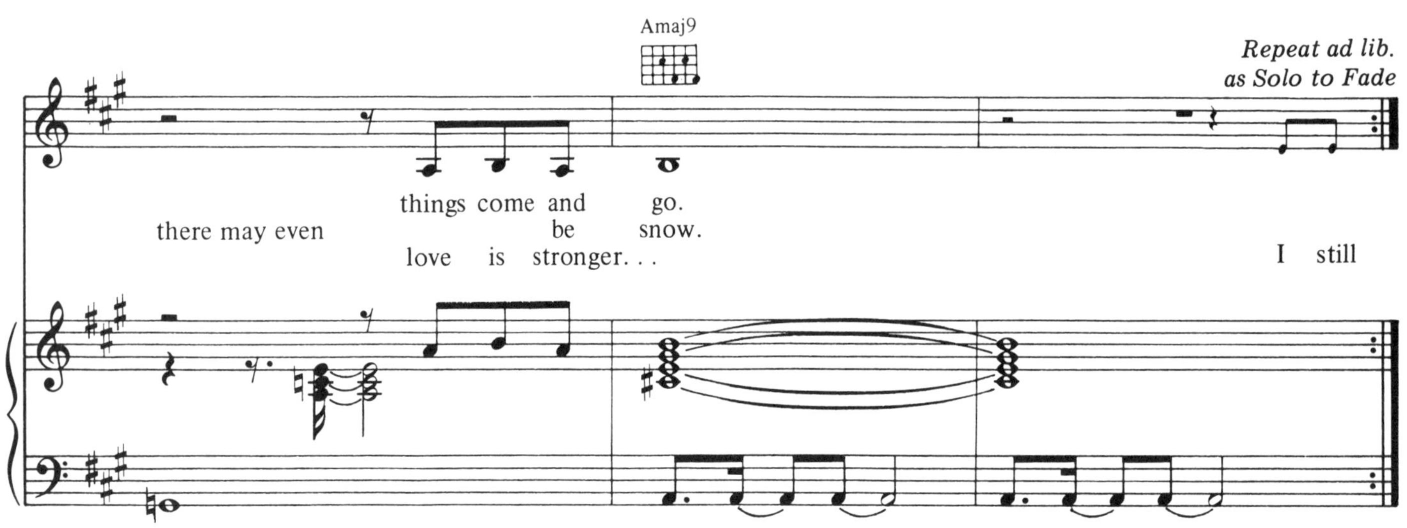
Amaj9
Repeat ad lib.
as Solo to Fade
things come and go.
there may even be snow.
love is stronger. . . I still

Paradise

Words & Music: Adu, Hale, Matthewman & Denman

Fm7
B♭/F
Fm7
mine.
Blow you right to my door,
B♭/F
Fm7
B♭/F
feels fine.
Fm7
B♭/F
Fm7
Feels like
you're mine,
feels right,
B♭/F
Fm7
so fine.
I'm yours,

B♭/F
Fm7
you're mine like pa-ra - dise.
B♭/F
Fm7
1.
B♭/F
Fm7
B♭/F
I'd give you the world if it was
Fm7
B♭/F
Fm7
mine.

Bb/F
Fm7
Bb/F
Feels fine.
Fm7
Bb/F
Fm7
Feels like
you're mine,
I'm yours,
Bb/F
Fm7
so fine,
like pa - ra - dise.
Bb/F
Fm7
Bb/F
I'd wash the

2.
Bb/F
Fm7
Bb/F
Ooh ___ what a life,
ooh ___
Fm7
1.
Bb/F
2.
Bb/F
what a life.
Ooh ___
I wan-na
Fm7
Bb/F
share my life, ___ I wan-na share my life ___ with you. ___ I wan-na
Fm7
Bb/F
(Gmaj7)
Repeat to Fade
share my life. ___
I wan- na

Nothing can come between us

Words & Music: Adu, Matthewman & Hale

Bbm7
Fm9
Bbm7
- der, so hold on.
- ness hold on.
Fm9
Bbm7
Fm9
In the mid-dle of the mad-ness when the time is run-ning out
So it tru-ly is a good thing and I al-ways wan-ted
Bbm7
Fm9
Bbm7
and you're left a-lone; all I want is you to know that it's
you to know there is al-ways this and this is ev-er-last-ing, hold
Fm9
1.
Bbm7
Fm9
strong still can't pull us a-part. Noth-ing can
on. (Counter) Noth-ing can come,

Bbm7
Fm9
Bbm7
Bbo
come be-tween us. Noth-ing can pull us a-part
Noth-ing can come, Noth-ing can come be-tween us. Yeah ba-by
Fm9
Bbm7
Fm9
can come be-tween us.
noth-ing can come noth-ing can come, noth-ing can come be-tween
Bbm7
2.
Bbm7
Fm9
It's a-bout faith,
us.
Bbm7
Fm9
Bbm7
Bbo
it's a-bout trust, (yeah yeah.) It's a-bout

Fm9
Bbm7
Fm9
faith,
it's a-bout trust.
Bbm7
Bbo
Fm9
Bbm7
Fm9
Bbm7
Fm9
1. 2. Noth-ing can come,
3. come,
4. pull
Bbm7
Fm9
Bbm7
Repeat to Fade
noth-ing can come,
noth-ing can come
be - tween us.
can tear,
us a - part.
(2o) Can
(3o) can

No ordinary love

Words & Music: Adu & Matthewman

F♯m7/B
Bm
that I have in - side and you took my love, you took my love.
1.
Bm7
Bm
B sus2 sus4
Did - n't I tell you what I be - lieve. Did some - bo - dy
Gmaj7/B
Em7/B
say that a love like that won't last. Did - n't I give you all that I've
F♯m7/B
Bm
Bm7
got to give ba - by?
3

2.
Bm7
Bm
Bsus2 sus4
I keep cry - ing,
I keep try -
Gmaj7/B
Em7/B
- ing for you.
There's no-thing like
F♯m7/B
Bm
Bm7
you and I,
ba - by.
This is no
Bm
Bsus2 sus4
Gmaj7/B
or - di - na-ry love,
no or - di - na - ry love.

Em7/B
F♯m7/B
This is no or - di - na - ry love, no or - di - na - ry love.
Bm
Bm7
To Coda
Bm
When you came my way
B sus2 sus4
Gmaj7/B
Em7/B
you bright - ened ev - 'ry day with
F♯m7/B
Bm
your sweet smile.

Bm7
Bm
Did - n't I tell you what I be -
B sus2 sus4
Gmaj7/B
lieve. Did some - bo - dy say that a
Em7/B
love like that won't last. Did - n't I give you all that I've
F♯m7/B
Bm
got to give, ba - by?

Bm7
Bm
2º instrumental
This is no or - di - na - ry love,
B sus2 sus4
Gmaj7/B
no or - di - na - ry love.
Em7/B
This is no or - di - na - ry love,
F♯m7/B
Bm
no or - di - na - ry love.

1.
2.
Bm7
Bm7
D.%. al Coda
I keep cry -
Coda
Bm
B sus2 sus4
Gmaj7/B
Em7/B
F♯m7/B
Bm
Bm7
Repeat to fade

Like a tattoo

Words & Music: Adu, Hale & Matthewman

Fm9
Cm7
fr3
truth.
And he spoke of his dreams,
Fm7/B♭
Cm9
bro-ken by the bur-den,
bro-ken by the bur-den of his
3
Fm9
Cm7
fr3
Fm7/B♭
youth.
Cm9
Fm9
Four-teen

Cm7
fr3
Fm7/B♭
3
years, he said,
I could - n't look in - to the sun.
Cm9
Fm9
E♭m9
fr4
She saw him lay - ing at the end of my gun.
Hun - gry for life and
Gm9
fr3
E♭m9
fr4
thir - sty for the dis - tant ri - ver.
Fm7/B♭
E♭m9
fr4
I re - mem - ber his hands and the way the moun -

Gm9
fr3
E♭m9
fr4
Fm7/B♭
3
-tains looked. The light shot dia-monds from his eyes. Hun-gry for
E♭m9
Gm9
life and thir-sty for the dis-tant ri - ver.
Cm7
Cm9
1, 2.
3.
Fm9
Like the scar of

E♭m9
Gm9
E♭m9
age writ- ten all ov - er my face. The war is still rag- ing in- side-
Fm7/B♭
E♭m9
of me. I still feel the chill as I re- veal my
Gm9
E♭m9
shame to you. I wear it like a tat-
Fm7/B♭
E♭m9
Fm7/B♭
Repeat to fade
too. I wear it like a tat - too. I

Kiss of life

Words & Music: Adu, Matthewman, Hale & Denman

Amaj7
F♯m7
There must have been an an - gel by my side, some - thing hea - ven - ly came
Dmaj7
C♯m7
fr4
Bm7
down from a - bove He led me to you, he
F♯m7
Bm7
led me to you. He built a
F♯m7
Bm7
F♯m11
fr4
3
bridge to your heart, all the way. How ma - ny

Bm7
F♯m7
To Coda
Bm7
tons of love in - side? I can't say.
F♯m11
fr4
Amaj7
When I was led to you, I
F♯m7
Dmaj7
C♯m7
fr4
Bm7
knew you were the one for me. I swear, the whole world
F♯m7
could feel my heart - beat. When

Amaj7
F♯m7
I lay eyes on you, ay, ay, ay,
Dmaj7
C♯m7
fr4
Bm7
you wrapped me up in the
F♯m7
Bm7
col - our of love. You gave me the kiss of life,
F♯m7
Bm7
F♯m11
fr4
kiss of life. You

Bm7
F♯m7
Bm7
gave me the kiss that's like the kiss of life.
F♯m11
fr4
Amaj7
1º instrumental
Was - n't it clear from the start?
F♯m7
Dmaj7
C♯m7
fr4
Bm7
Look, the sky is full of love. Yeah, the sky
F♯m7
D.%. al Coda
2º only
is full of love. He

Coda
Bm7
F♯m11
fr4
say.
You
Bm7
Instrumental from 3º
F♯m7
Bm7
gave me the kiss of life,
kiss of life.
F♯m11
fr4
Bm7
You gave me the kiss that's like
F♯m7
Bm7
F♯11
fr4
Repeat to fade
the kiss of life.
You

Please send me someone to love

Words & Music: Percy Mayfield

A9 fr6
B9 C9 B9
please send me some - one to love.
Show all the
E6 E13 fr6 E7/G♯ E7 A7
world how to get a - long, peace will en - ter when
B♭dim7 F♯7 E/B B♭m7(♭5)
hate is gone. But, if it's not ask - ing too much,
A7 B7 E E6 E E7
please send me some - one to love.
I lay a -

A13 Am7 E E7
fr5
wake nights and pon - der world trou - bles. My
F♯m9 B13 E6 E7
ans - wer is al - ways the same. That un -
A Am9 E C♯7 aug F♯7
fr5 fr4
less men put an end to all of this, hate will put the world in a
B7 aug E6 E7 D/F♯ E7/G♯ E7
2º instrumental
flame, what a shame. Just be - cause I'm in mi- se - ry I'm not beg-

A7
B♭dim7
F♯7
E/B
B♭m7(♭5)
ging for no sym-pa-thy. But, if it's not ask-ing too much,
A7
B7
E6
1.
please send me some-one to love.
2.
E6
D.%. al Coda
Coda
E/B
B♭m7(♭5)
Hea-ven,
not ask-ing too much,
A7
B7
E
F♯m7
Em7/G
F♯m7
E
please send me some-one to love.
Hm-m-mm.

Cherish the day

Words & Music: Adu, Hale & Matthewman

♩= 80
Cm7
fr3
Dm7/C
Fm7/C
1.
Gm7/C
2.
Gm7/C
Cm7
fr3
You're rul - ing the way that I move,
Dm7/C
Fm7/C
Gm7/C
and I breath your air.
You on- ly can

Cm7
fr3
Dm7/C
Fm7/C
res- cue me,
this is my prayer.
Gm7/C
Cm7
fr3
2º instrumental
Dm7/C
If you were mine,
Fm7/C
Gm7/C
Cm7
fr3
if you were mine,
I would - n't want to go
Dm7/C
Fm7/C
Gm7/C
Sing both times
3
to hea - ven.
I che - rish the
3

Cm7
fr3
Dm7/C
day, I won't go a - stray, I won't be a -
Fm7/C
To Coda
Gm7/C
fraid, you won't catch me run - ning. You're rul - ing the
Cm7
fr3
Dm7/C
way that I move, you take my air,
Fm7/C
Gm7/C
Cm7
fr3
you show me how deep love can be.

Dm7/C
Fm7/C
Gm7/C
D.C. al Coda
Coda
Gm7/C
Cm7
fr3
run - ning. I che - rish the day, I won't go a -
Dm7/C
Fm7/C
stray, I won't be a - fraid, won't run a -
Gm7/C
B♭/C
1º no chord
way.
R.H. tacet 1º

Tacet 1º
Cm7
fr3
You show me how deep love can be.
Dm7/C
Fm7/C
Gm7/C
You show me how
Cm7
fr3
deep love can be.
Dm7/C
Fm7/C
This is my prayer.
Gm7/C
Cm7
fr3
I che - rish the day, I won't go a -

Dm7/C
Fm7/C
stray, I won't be a - fraid, won't
Gm7/C
Cm7
fr3
Dm7/C
run a-way, won't shy. I che-rish the day, I won't go a - stray.
Fm7/C
Gm7/C
Cm7
fr3
I che-rish the day.
Dm7/C
Fm7/C
Gm7/C
Repeat to fade
I che-rish the day.

Pearls

Words & Music: Adu & Hale

♩= 52
Gm7
fr3
F6/9
E♭maj9
fr5
pedal throughout
D7sus4
D7
D7(♯9)
fr4
There is a woman in So - ma - lia
scrap-ing for pearls on the road - side. There's a force strong - er than na - ture,

D7sus4
D7
Gm7
fr3
keeps her will a - live.
This is how she's dy - ing,
she's
F6/9
E♭maj9
fr5
dy - ing to sur - vive.
Don't know what she's made of,
I would
D7sus4
D7
Cm9
like to be that brave.
She cries to the hea - ven a - bove,
Dm7
Cm9
there is a stone in my heart.

Dm7
Cm9
She lives a life she did - n't choose
Dm7
Cm9
and it hurts like brand new shoes,
Dm7
D7
Gm7
fr3
hurts like brand new shoes.
To Coda
F6/9
E♭maj9
fr5
D7sus4
D7
There is a

Gm7
fr3
F6/9
woman in So-ma-lia, the sun gives her no mer-cy. The
E♭maj9
fr5
D7sus4
D7
3
same sky we lay un-der burns her to the bone. Long as
Gm7
fr3
F6/9
3
af-ter-noon sha-dows, it's gon-na take her to get home.
E♭maj9
fr5
D7sus4
D7
3
Each grain care-ful-ly wrapped up, pearls for her lit-tle girl. Hal-le-

Gm7
fr3
F6/9
3
lu - - - - - - jah.
Hal - le -
E♭maj9
fr5
D7sus4
D7
D.%. al Coda
lu - - - - - - jah.
She cries to the
Coda
D7sus4
D7
Gm7
fr3
F6/9
E♭maj9
fr5
D7sus4
D7
Gm
fr3

7/96 (24845)